So Cute! Baby Animals

Donkeys

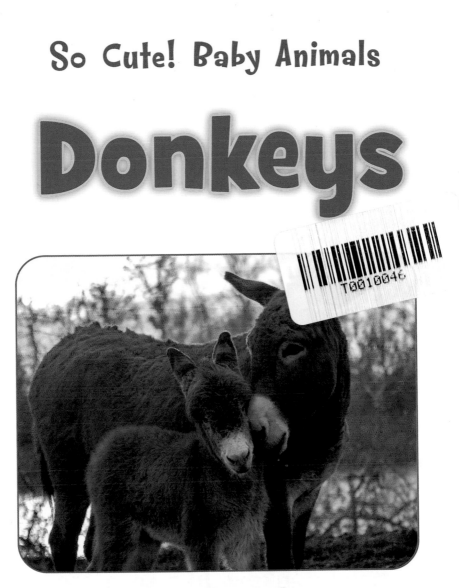

By Julia Jaske

 Baby donkeys like to graze.

Baby donkeys like to eat.

Baby donkeys like to bray.

Baby donkeys like to explore.

Baby donkeys like to walk.

Baby donkeys like to sniff.

Baby donkeys like to smile.

Baby donkeys like to hug.

Baby donkeys like to jump.

Baby donkeys like to trot.

Baby donkeys like to play.

Baby donkeys like to sleep.

Word List

Baby	explore	jump
donkeys	walk	trot
graze	sniff	play
eat	smile	sleep
bray	hug	

60 Words

Baby donkeys like to graze.
Baby donkeys like to eat.
Baby donkeys like to bray.
Baby donkeys like to explore.
Baby donkeys like to walk.
Baby donkeys like to sniff.
Baby donkeys like to smile.
Baby donkeys like to hug.
Baby donkeys like to jump.
Baby donkeys like to trot.
Baby donkeys like to play.
Baby donkeys like to sleep.

CHERRY BLOSSOM PRESS

Published in the United States of America by Cherry Lake Publishing Group
Ann Arbor, Michigan
www.cherrylakepublishing.com

Book Designer: Melinda Millward

Photo Credits: © Budimir Jevtic/Shutterstock, cover, 1; © Valerio951/Shutterstock, 2; © sisqopote/Shutterstock, 3; © Geza Farkas/Shutterstock, 4; © Tami Freed/Shutterstock, 5; © Don Fink/Shutterstock, 6; © Alena A/Shutterstock, 7; © Blue Iris/Shutterstock, 8; © Ruslana Iurchenko/Shutterstock, 9; © George Marcel/Shutterstock, 10; © Agarianna76/Shutterstock, 11; © CLS Digital Arts/Shutterstock, 12; © DejaVuDesigns/Shutterstock, 13; © Eric Isselee/Shutterstock, 14

Cherry Blossom Press is an imprint of Cherry Lake Publishing Group.

Library of Congress Cataloging-in-Publication Data

Names: Jaske, Julia, author.
Title: Donkeys / written by Julia Jaske.
Description: Ann Arbor, Michigan : Cherry Lake Publishing, [2022] | Series: So cute! Baby animals
Identifiers: LCCN 2022009894 | ISBN 9781668908785 (paperback) | ISBN 9781668911976 (ebook) | ISBN 9781668913567 (pdf)
Subjects: LCSH: Donkeys—Infancy—Juvenile literature.
Classification: LCC SF361 .J37 2022 | DDC 636.1/8207—dc23/eng/20220330
LC record available at https://lccn.loc.gov/2022009894

Cherry Lake Publishing Group would like to acknowledge the work of the Partnership for 21st Century Learning, a Network of Battelle for Kids. Please visit http://www.battelleforkids.org/networks/p21 for more information.

Printed in the United States of America
Corporate Graphics